THE
GHOSTLY TALES
OF

PUT-IN-BAY

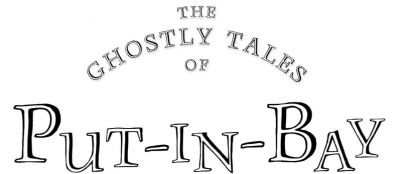

Published by Arcadia Children's Books
A Division of Arcadia Publishing
Charleston, SC
www.arcadiapublishing.com

Spooky America is a trademark of Arcadia Publishing, Inc.

First published 2022

Manufactured in the United States

ISBN 978-1-4671-9870-7

Library of Congress Control Number: 2022932228

All images courtesy of Shutterstock.com.

Notice: The information in this book is true and complete to the best of our knowledge. It is offered without guarantee on the part of the author or Arcadia Publishing. The author and Arcadia Publishing disclaim all liability in connection with the use of this book.

THE

GHOSTLY TALES

OF

PUT-IN-BAY

JAY WHISTLER

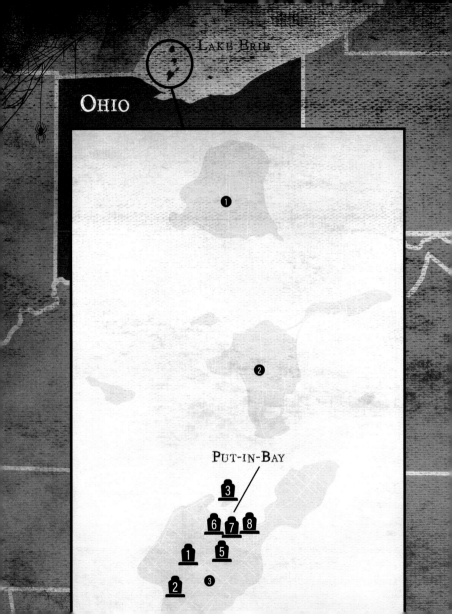

LAKE ERIE

OHIO

PUT-IN-BAY

TABLE OF CONTENTS & MAP KEY

1 North Bass Island

2 Middle Bass Island

3 South Bass Island

* Put-in-Bay is a township on South Bass Island, in Ohio. It is also the name of the small bay where the township is built. It is *also* the name used to refer to the three islands shown here: North Bass Island, Middle Bass Island, and South Bass Island.

Introduction

What kind of name is Put-in-Bay? Say it fast and it sounds like "puddin'." But why would someone name this Ohio lake-view outpost after a dessert?

There are several theories about the origins of the name. A map from the 1750s shows a newly charted "Pudding Bay," perhaps because it resembled a "pudding bag." Long ago, pudding described a variety of slow-cooked concoctions of dried fruits, sugar, rum, flour, nuts, and spices shaped into a ball, wrapped into a muslin square tied at the top, then simmered in water for about six hours until cooked through. When the pudding was done, it was lifted out of the water, and the fabric cut away to reveal a glistening dome that was sliced and topped with a sweet sauce. The bundle and its contents are what early explorers may have envisioned when they saw the shape of the bay.

Another theory is the bay provided shelter from storms. Although the island surrounding the bay was uninhabited until the late 1700s, it offered plenty of covered spaces, including a cave, for crews to find safety during gales. So, sailors named the bay to signal to other vessels this was a safe place to "put in."

Put-in-Bay is also confusing from a different perspective. Many people think it refers to the city on the edge of the bay or to the island itself.

Actually, Put-in-Bay is the name of the body of water, while the island itself is called South Bass Island and is one of the three Bass Islands in Lake Erie, which also includes Middle Bass and North Bass Islands. Together, the three islands make up the township of Put-in-Bay. The confusion doesn't end there because there is also the village of Put-in-Bay, which is the small town surrounding the bay itself.

So, we have Put-in-Bay, the body of water; Put-in-Bay Village on its shores; and Put-in-Bay Township, encompassing South, Middle, and North Bass Islands. But if you simply say, "Put-in-Bay," most people know what you mean.

Put-in-Bay has many attractions. If you're into fishing, grab your rod and reel, pick up a fishing license, and try your luck with some of the best spots in the United States for perch and walleye. If you'd rather study your fish up close, head to the Put-in-Bay Aquatic Center. Operated through The Ohio State University, the center boasts hands-on activities for children and adults alike.

Be sure to tour Perry's Cave, which sits 52 feet below Lake Erie. Here you can see stalactites, stalagmites, and cave pearls in the 208-foot-long chamber. You can watch as the underground lake rises and falls in sync with Lake Erie.

Perhaps you prefer being more of a hands-on rockhound. Check out Put-in-Bay Gemstone mining, where you can search for fossils, geodes, and gemstones by panning for them the way miners used to. Or visit Crystal Cave to see the world's largest geode.

Put-in-Bay is home to one of the last surviving carousels of the early 20th century. Opening around 1917, Kimberly's Carousel was built by the world-renowned Allan Herschell

Company, famous for its intricately carved and brightly painted animals. Of the over 3,000 carousels made by the Herschell Company, only 148 still exist in the United States and Canada. But Kimberly's Carousel is the only one that lays claim to the famous "Petey the Perch." If you go, be sure to reel him in before any of the other riders can!

While there are plenty of activities to fill your lazy summer days, Put-in-Bay has quite the history. Did you know a famous US Navy slogan originated from this area? That's just one of the interesting facts that make Put-in-Bay such a special—and spooky—place. Let's take a tour around the bay and find out more!

The First Explorers

Let's begin our ghost tour over two thousand years ago, before colonists arrived in what we know as Ohio, Michigan, Indiana, and Illinois; before Native Americans became the dominant population; even before any permanent encampment was established. The first evidence historians have of civilization in the Lake Erie region dates from approximately 1000 BCE to 1200 CE, when the area was covered in thick stands of oak, hickory, elm, cottonwood, and maple trees. Cattails, grasses, and sedges lined the shores of Lake Erie and the Bass Island chain.

Nuts from trees, fish, and weaving materials from the water plants made the islands an important resource for what archaeologists call the Mound Builders, several groups of indigenous people who together inhabited the region. Because of their nomadic ways, scholars have had a difficult time learning about their lives, and everything we know today comes from the earthen mounds the Mound Builders left behind.

There are several known types of mounds, including burial, effigy (made to resemble an animal or spirit), and ceremonial. Built into  the ground, they typically consisted of topsoil, clay, animal bones, and other organic material. Burial mounds seem to have been used exclusively for elders or important members of the community. In Ohio, most of the skeletons found in burial mounds are males. These mounds contained the body, religious or ceremonial paraphernalia, and items belonging to the deceased.

Unfortunately, these clues provide little DNA evidence to help scientists figure out where the Mound Builders arrived from or where they went after they left the area. Many of the original mounds were destroyed when European settlers found their way to the island, and artifacts were taken to Europe in the 1700s and 1800s, where they remain, unavailable to researchers who might be able to discover more. However, from the little researchers know, it seems unlikely these groups resided on any of the Bass Islands. Instead, researchers guess the Mound Builders used the islands as hunting grounds, specifically for raccoons, which were plentiful in those days. They also fished there, likely for walleye and perch, just as modern humans do.

After the Mound Builders faded away, they were replaced by the Erie, the earliest known Native American group, who are likely to have been dominant until the mid-1600s, when the Iroquois confederation defeated the Erie for control. By the early 1700s, the Shawnee, Miami, Seneca, Wyandot, Delaware, and Pottawatomie (POT-ah-WAD-uh-me) peoples all had a presence in the region. Evidence shows these groups used the islands as a shelter. Researchers have found evidence of early campfires, carbon-dated to well before the first settlers arrived. Depending on the construction, canoes and kayaks wouldn't be able to survive the stormy waters while the

Native Americans were out fishing, traveling to other islands for food, or trading with other nations, and the campfires suggest Native Americans built them to stay warm during storms, or perhaps to signal to the mainland they were stuck on the island.

There is also archaeological evidence to suggest Native Americans used a cave on South Bass Island, now called Perry's Cave, because of its unique underground pond with a constant supply of freshwater. They may have also stored food there because the cave

is always a cool 50 degrees, even in winter. To date, eight skeletons have been discovered in the cave. Analysis led researchers to estimate the height of the bodies to all be nearly seven feet tall! Who knew Put-in-Bay was originally the land of the giants? Maybe it was something in that water.

Occasionally, tourists in Perry's Cave have said their photos taken inside the cavern show shafts of light where there are no openings to the outside. Could it be possible the ghosts of Native Americans past are responsible for the eerie floating campfires often seen over South and Middle Bass Islands? Or maybe they are the visual echoes of Erie or Iroquois hunters, trying in vain to signal for rescue or light their way in the stormy darkness.

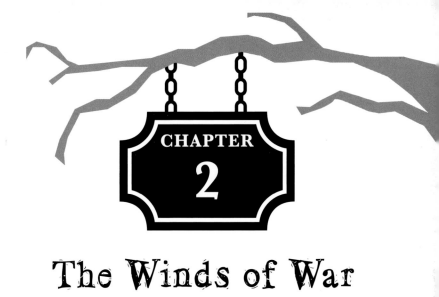

The Winds of War

In the mid-1600s, Native Americans knew the area so well, they had established settlements, hunting ranges, subsistence farming, and trade routes among the different groups. To colonists, however, Ohio and its Lake Erie shoreline were considered untamed wilderness because the land and water had yet to be explored by Europeans. In 1669, all that changed when a French-Canadian explorer named Louis Jolliet arrived in the Lake Erie area near South Bass Island and Put-in-Bay, according to most historians. He began charting waterways in the Upper Midwest, including both Michigan peninsulas, Wisconsin, and Ohio. He was also the first man to thoroughly chart the Upper Mississippi River valley. Ten years later, another explorer, René-Robert Cavelier—also known as Sir LaSalle—claimed the entire Mississippi River valley, including the Ohio River valley, in the name of King Louis XIV of France.

Yet, for nearly a hundred years after Jolliet and La Salle's explorations, colonists still did not filter into Northern Ohio in large numbers. The area, though now charted, was still seen as the outer reaches of the continent, and most British colonists remained in the original colonies, while French colonists settled in the Canadian territories of Novia Scotia and New Brunswick.

In the mid-1700s, French colonists made claim to the Ohio River valley, citing the history of French explorers in the region, particularly that of Sir LaSalle. Their alliances with the indigenous peoples of America and Canada through the French fur trade only bolstered their position. Great Britain, however, under the rule of King George II, claimed right to the same land, referencing a series of royal charters granted by the British monarchy in the 1600s. These tensions led to the French and Indian War in 1754, as an outnumbered French army managed to fight back American colonial forces. The American army was still young, untrained, and lacking support from Great Britain. Not until King George II realized he was in danger of losing the colonies to the

French did he send reinforcements to support the American colonists.

Once the British Army arrived, the tide of the French and Indian War changed. Not only were the British troops more organized and better armed than their colonial brothers in arms, but they also had more money than the French army. They were a war machine. Though it took a few more years of hostilities, the British prevailed, and both sides signed the Treaty of Paris in the French capital on February 10, 1763.

The French and Indian War had been expensive, and King George II imposed hefty taxes on the colonies to help pay his war debt. As a result, the colonists felt taken advantage of because they had no representation in the British government and therefore no one to stand up for their interests. Instead, the colonies had all the responsibilities of British citizens, but none of the rights. Not only did they lack a voice in government, but Britain could demand that colonists house, feed, and maintain British troops with no financial compensation. Colonists were not entitled to a trial by jury, nor could they assemble in protest.

The First Continental Congress assembled in September 1774 and sent a list of grievances to the crown, the most important of which was taxation without representation. The crown responded by sending in more troops to bring the colonies to heel.

On April 18, 1775, the British marched from Boston to Concord, Massachusetts, to seize weapons stockpiled by the colonists, marking the beginning of the American Revolutionary War.

The fledgling Continental Army would battle the British for eight long and brutal years until Britain finally recognized American independence on September 3, 1783.

The long war was finally over.

Although several battles were fought on Ohio soil during this time, the war prevented westward colonial expansion. Between the French and Indian War and the Revolutionary War, Ohio's population grew minimally during those thirty-nine years, and South Bass Island and Put-in-Bay remained largely uninhabited. But all that was about to change.

The Battle of Lake Erie

Did you know Put-in-Bay and South Bass Island were once part of Connecticut? In 1662, King Charles II of England granted the colony the land between the 41st and 42nd parallels from "sea to sea," meaning Connecticut owned the sliver from the Atlantic to the Pacific.

After the Revolutionary War ended in 1783, some colonies squabbled over who controlled the land, especially around the Great Lakes.

The waterways, they knew, would provide excellent economic resources, and allow for expanded trade routes.

The newly formed federal government realized the bickering could lead to civil war. So, they insisted any colony wishing to be part of the new republic must turn over all rights to any land charters to the federal government. In exchange, colonies received all the rights and privileges of membership in the republic.

The deal was too good to pass up, and in 1786, Connecticut signed over their sea-to-sea rights. They were allowed to keep a small portion they divided and gave to citizens who suffered losses during the Revolution. The remaining territory was sold to the Connecticut Land Company in 1795.

These days, we think of Washington state and Oregon as the Northwest. But in 1787, the Northwestern Ordinance established what was known as the Northwest Territories. It encompassed what is now Ohio, Michigan, Indiana, Illinois, Wisconsin, and the northeastern corner of Minnesota. Sixteen years later, President Thomas Jefferson signed an Act of Congress on February 19, 1803, declaring Ohio the seventeenth state in the union.

In 1807, a Connecticut congressman named Pierpont Edwards decided to purchase land from the Connecticut Land Company. Due to a legal technicality, the borders of Edwards's purchase were in question. As a compromise, the company granted Edwards South Bass Island and Put-in-Bay.

In 1811, Edwards sent a crew to survey the island and determine a suitable use for it. The crew cleared over 100 acres of trees to create farmland. They also imported sheep and hogs who fed on the abundant acorns and hickory nuts. Families settled on the island to find prosperity as farmers.

But the War of 1812 brought British troops to the island. They destroyed all the crops, seized livestock to feed their armies, and forced farmers to flee. South Bass Island was once again largely uninhabited. The War of 1812 was significant for the region because for most of the war, the British controlled the Great Lakes, except for Lake Huron. Without this control, it seemed unlikely the United States could ever defeat the might of the British Navy, once considered the most powerful naval force in the world.

That is, until Commander Oliver Hazard Perry won a pivotal battle on Lake Erie, changing the war's outcome. Because of Put-in-Bay's shape, Commander Perry and his ships used it as a base for his fleet. In the bay, approaching ships could be spotted easily and dispatched quickly. The bay's location allowed Perry to travel swiftly to meet other navy officers to plan battles and discuss strategies or resupply ships.

Perry's fleet had two flagships, the USS *Niagara* and the USS *Lawrence*. The *Lawrence* was the namesake of a fallen naval captain and close friend of Perry's named James Lawrence, whose ship took on heavy cannon fire in June of 1813, and the captain worried it would be surrendered. Lawrence, mortally wounded, gave his men one last order: "Don't give up the ship." That motto appeared on a pennant hoisted on the USS *Lawrence* in honor of the fallen hero.

On September 10, 1813, The Battle of Lake Erie tested the US Navy's strength. The USS *Lawrence*, captained by Commander Perry himself, took on heavy fire from the British navy and was all but destroyed. Perry saved the pennant honoring his comrade, and he and the surviving crew abandoned ship and rowed to the nearby USS *Niagara*, where Perry assumed command.

Through a series of strategic maneuvers, Perry disabled nearly all the enemies' vessels, and the British surrendered after the nearly eight-hour battle. At the end of the fighting, Perry sent a message to General William Henry Harrison, the leader of the Army of the Northwest, a US Army unit formed at the beginning of the war to oversee the land campaign in the Northwest Territories. In the message, Perry said, "We have met the enemy and they are ours." While not an official

motto—the Navy doesn't have one—Perry's words to Harrison have become an unofficial US Navy slogan.

Though there is no written proof, it is rumored Perry once housed British prisoners of war down in Perry's Cave. Could the lights people claim to see in the depths of the cave be the memories of the prisoners' candlelight as they lived in near-total darkness during their captivity? Or maybe it is the reflection of long-extinguished campfires prisoners made to chase away the constant chill and damp fifty feet below the earth. Whatever the cause, visit Perry's Cave yourself and see if you can discover the source of the glow. And the breeze on the back of your neck? It might just be one of Perry's prisoners exhaling a frigid breath to get your attention.

Seen from the air, South Bass Island looks vaguely like a guitar, with an oddly shaped body to the southwest, a stubby headstock to the northeast, and a short neck between them. Part of the National Park Service, Perry's Victory and International Peace Memorial takes up the entire neck of the guitar, joining the two sections of the island.

The 352-foot Doric column, erected between 1912 and 1915, was built to recognize the 100th anniversary of the Battle of Lake Erie and as a memorial to the peace the United States, Canada, and Great Britain have shared ever since the war ended. A list of names on the facade of the memorial commemorates the thirty-four men who died in the fighting or succumbed to their injuries and the ninety-six wounded.

A small, separate building sits to the west of the memorial. The Ranger Operation Center, also known as "the Roc," is a small one-story facility that originally provided showers for the nearby beach. Today, National

Park Service rangers use the building as an administrative hub.

Before the memorial was completed, it had several brush encounters with death, one could say. To start, the remains of six naval officers killed during the Battle of Lake Erie were exhumed from a local burial site and relocated under the foundation of the memorial. The construction of the monument also resulted in two casualties: Antonio Fabianto and George Cochran both died several months apart in 1914. It was also the scene of the tragic death of a young Michigan woman, Betty Lester, in 1945.

Paranormal investigators believe some hauntings are like a video of an event playing on an endless loop. A ranger named Martin shared what he experienced on his first day working the ticket desk at the elevator leading to the observation deck, an experience that might be like that of a paranormal video loop. It was the off-season, so the lobby was rather empty. As he read a book during a quiet moment, the ranger heard a loud bang across the lobby. He looked up to see one of the velvet ropes used to guide visitors to the desk had been thrown across the room, where it lay like a snake in front of the elevator. The rope was about six feet away from the stanchion it should have been connected to. Martin replaced the rope and checked to make sure the lobby was truly empty. As he suspected, he was quite alone. Or was he?

Martin may not have been familiar with the tragic story of Betty Lester. On a boat trip with her sister and a friend to visit Cedar Point, the group made a stop at South Bass Island. When it came time to leave, eighteen-year-old Betty was nowhere to be found. Helen, her fifteen-year-old sister, assumed Betty wanted to stay on the island. So, the boat continued to Cedar Point without Betty. When the boat returned to the island later that same evening, Betty still didn't show up. After arriving home in Hazel Park, her family reported her missing. The next morning, Mr. Lester arrived in Put-in-Bay, and authorities let him know his daughter had taken her own life by jumping from the tower's observation platform, 317 feet above lake level. Mr. Lester said his daughter had dealt with mental health issues for the last eighteen months and had gone through several periods of deep depression.

While we may never know what was going through Betty's mind, perhaps she still walks the halls of the tower today. Maybe she was in a hurry to reach the elevator as she breezed past the ranger and tossed the rope out of her way in her haste.

There may be another explanation:

Antonio Fabianto died when construction debris fell on him near the base of the tower, and construction equipment landed on George Cochran a few months later in nearly the same spot. Perhaps the disturbance in the lobby was a ghostly loop of something falling. Ghost hunters have searched tirelessly for the cause, but the source is still unknown.

In another incident, a ranger watched a person walk along the maintenance level above the elevator. This level, with its open walkway, is not accessible to visitors. Park rangers access it via a hidden stairway, but only with a key. Even if someone managed to find and unlock the door, there is another locked gate at the top of the stairs.

On this day, the ranger was helping a school tour group when he noticed someone on the maintenance level. Because the hallway is in shadows, he couldn't see who it was or what they wore, though the clothing appeared dark. Once the tour group was situated, the ranger contacted maintenance to find out who was up there. The maintenance supervisor insisted no work was scheduled for the area. Concerned it may be a park guest who somehow gained access, the ranger searched the maintenance level but found no one there.

The ranger is not the only person to have witnessed someone walking along this level. Guests occasionally ask the desk ranger who is up there. But when they look again, the person is gone. All these sightings happen when no maintenance is scheduled.

One theory is the naval officers whose remains are under the memorial's foundation patrol this level, scanning the horizon for enemy ships. In their dark uniforms, they continue to protect our country, even in death.

Rangers and visitors alike share stories

of overhearing raised voices when no one is nearby. The voices are clear and seem to be arguing about war strategy or politics. Some observers believe the men are the veterans of the Battle of Lake Erie, heatedly discussing battle plans or strained international relations. Others surmise the men may be the ghosts of both US and British military. It seems several the British casualties of the Battle of Lake Erie were interred in a nearby cemetery rather than being buried "at sea" in the lake, as was the custom in both the US and British navies. One researcher thinks the remains in the foundation might include one or more British sailors, and this is the source of the ghostly tension heard near the memorial.

While it was not originally part of the memorial and served no military purpose in its former life, the Roc has seen ghostly activity, too. Rangers working alone in the building often hear unexplained footsteps and report a strong feeling of being watched, a prickly sensation arising on the hair on the back of their necks. None of the rangers believe these presences are malevolent. Instead, they may be the spirits of long-ago beachgoers revisiting a place they felt happy.

If you visit Perry's Victory and International Peace Memorial, listen for sailors arguing with one another. Or maybe you'll be lucky enough to see one of our brave fighting men patrol the maintenance level of the tower. And if you happen to feel someone watching you near the Roc, remember it's probably just someone reliving their visits to the beach over one hundred years ago.

Finally . . . Peace

By the time the War of 1812 ended in 1815, first the colonies, and then the United States had been at war off and on for sixty-one years. South Bass Island had seen barely any settlers on its shores.

Pierpont Edwards tried to settle the island again during the War of 1812 and sent his eldest son, John Stark Edwards, to survey the damage left by the British. But the younger

Edwards made it as far as the Marblehead Peninsula, a mere nine-mile boat journey short of his destination, where he died of yellow fever on February 11, 1813.

When peace arrived in Ohio and the country, Edwards encouraged settlement on the island once more. In 1818, he sent another envoy to handle all legal, fiscal, and construction matters.

Several families responded to Edwards's encouragement, using the island's natural resources to build log-frame homes. They hunted raccoons, foxes, and feral hogs, descendants of the first hogs imported to the island in 1811. Fish were also plentiful, and word soon spread that the Bass Island chain was a hunter's and angler's paradise.

In 1823, the Edwards family built the first permanent timber-frame home on the island as a summer getaway. Edwards himself would never set eyes on his property, however, and died in 1826. He left all his property to his surviving son, Henry Alfred Pierpont Edwards. Also known as A.P., the younger Edwards owned the islands until his daughter, Alice, married Elisha Dyer Vinton on October 19, 1853, when he gifted his daughter and new son-in-law all three of the Bass Islands and several smaller islands. But Vinton wasn't interested in owning land. He asked his new father-in-law to sell the islands so Vinton and Alice could have the cash instead.

Edwards sold all three Bass Islands and four smaller islands to Joseph De Rivera St. Jurjo in 1854. At last, South Bass Island and Put-in-Bay truly began developing into the vacation destination we know today. But with all the people came more reports of haunted spaces.

Puerto Rican plantation owners José and Juana De Rivera were visiting family in Spain when their son, Joseph De Rivera, was born on

March 20, 1813. When Joseph was a year old, his parents returned to Puerto Rico, where he spent his youth. At the time, Puerto Rico was a Spanish colony. In 1898, a treaty with Spain granted the island to the US, and since then, all Puerto Ricans are legal US citizens.

In 1835, when he was 22, Mr. De Rivera moved to New York to start a successful trading company. In 1838, he became a US citizen. On his naturalization papers, Mr. De Rivera added "St. Jurjo" after his last name. He explained it was Spanish custom to use both parents' surnames, and thus his full legal name became Joseph De Rivera St. Jurjo. On some official records and in some reference material, the name is spelled "Jurgo," though it is unclear why. Regardless, to friends and colleagues, he was De Rivera.

For the next twenty years, Mr. De Rivera continued to build his trading company and started a land development venture. When A.P. Edwards advertised the Bass Islands for sale, Mr. De Rivera knew a good opportunity when he saw it, so he quickly agreed to buy everything for a total of $44,000, or about $1.5 million in today's dollars.

For the first few years, Mr. De Rivera established trade of all the islands' natural resources. He harvested lumber to use as steamboat fuel. He quarried gravel for building and road projects on the mainland. He farmed sheep and sold them on the New York commodities markets.

Now that the area's true economic value was widely known, Mr. De Rivera created numerous ten-acre land parcels. In a show of generosity, he sold the first parcel to the South Bass Island Board of Education for one dollar. The Board then established the first permanent school building on South Bass Island.

By 1864, Mr. De Rivera had sold forty-two ten-acre parcels. He was also a generous man and donated more land to the community for the island's schools, a local park, and St. Edward's Episcopal Church.

It was Mr. De Rivera who first realized the limestone-rich soil and temperate climate provided the perfect conditions for white-wine grapes, especially the Catawba, which the island is still known for. The year 1858 is known on South Bass Island as the "Year of the Grape" because that is when Mr. De Rivera introduced grapes to the island.

Winemaking became so successful, it sparked a boom in German immigrants to the area, many of whom were expert winemakers in the Rhineland wine region. Some even brought grapevines with them to the island. The Heineman Winery, established in 1896, managed to survive Prohibition and is now the oldest family-owned vineyard on the island.

Within a decade after the Year of the Grape, land prices surged from $10 to $1,500 per acre. South Bass Island and Put-in-Bay were really on the map now.

Mr. De Rivera's contributions to developing the Bass Islands, his visionary effort in creating a thriving wine industry, and his generous donations of land for schools, churches, parks, cemeteries, and more made him a beloved figure.

But Mr. De Rivera wasn't finished. His crowning achievement was guiding civic government to create Put-in-Bay Village, which was officially established in 1877. It's fitting, then, the park in the center of town bears his name, and a statue in his honor watches over the village he loved so dearly.

In 2017, a fierce storm rolled in from the lake and damaged a 200-year-old white oak. Instead of chopping the tree down, organizers hired a local woodworker to save the trunk and carve a larger-than-life likeness of the village founder. It was unveiled in May 2018.

Joseph De Rivera St. Jurjo died at Put-in-Bay in 1889 and was laid to rest in the cemetery he donated to the village.

If you visit the cemetery, maybe you will see Mr. De Rivera's spirit proudly gazing over

the modern community Put-in-Bay township and South Bass Island have become since his passing. After all, if not for him, the lovely island we know today would not look the same.

Prohibition

Did you know Canada is south of Michigan? It's true! Middle Island (not to be confused with Middle Bass Island), Canada's southernmost landmass, falls at 41.42 degrees latitude. Detroit, by comparison, sits at just over 42 degrees. While this might seem like merely an interesting geography tidbit, there's another reason it's important: Prohibition

In January 1920, the United States passed the 18th Amendment to the US Constitution, which prohibited the manufacture, transportation, or sale of alcohol throughout the country. For nearly fourteen years, until December 1933, when the 21st Amendment repealed the 18th amendment to end Prohibition, Americans didn't always obey the law. People all over the country built illegal distilleries to create gin, whiskey, vodka, and more. Ohio, because of its proximity to Canada, illegally imported alcohol from Ontario. The Detroit River and Lake Erie were the most common transportation routes. Couriers nicknamed "rumrunners" took boats back and forth, usually at night, and occasionally stopped on Pelee or Middle Islands to transfer their cargo to another vessel that continued the journey. In the winter, couriers even drove across the ice, a dangerous endeavor, indeed. Cars and trucks in the 1920s, though much lighter than modern vehicles, were heavy enough. Add on the extra weight of dozens, if not hundreds, of bottles of alcohol, not only did they run the risk of losing control on the ice, but many vehicles plunged through weak spots, never to be seen again.

One Put-in-Bay resident knows all about one of the tragedies. When the resident—let's call him "Ray"—was a teenager in the 1950s, he spent an afternoon ice-fishing on the lake. As evening descended, a snow squall blew in reducing visibility to near zero. Ray began the trek back to town, but the blinding snow blotted out the town's lights, and soon, he couldn't tell which way was home. As he was about to turn back to take shelter in his shanty, he spotted headlights on the ice, headed right toward him. He flagged the driver down and hopped in the vintage 1930s Ford. It wasn't uncommon in those days to see such an old vehicle because they were lighter than modern vehicles and still used for traveling on the ice. So, Ray didn't think it was out of the ordinary.

The driver introduced himself, Ray did the same, and off they headed toward town. Soon, the lights of the village appeared, and the driver stopped a few hundred yards from shore and said he hoped this was close enough. Grateful for the rescue, but with no cash on him, Ray offered the driver some of his fish. Instead, the driver pointed to the bottle of Heineman's Pink Catawba wine in Ray's hand and said he reckoned that would be payment enough. Ray handed over the bottle, said his farewells, and walked home.

When he arrived, he shared the story with his father, who asked the driver's name. Ray told him, but his father said it was impossible.

The man had died in 1930, over twenty years earlier, when his Ford plummeted through the ice. A rescue party never found the vehicle, but his body was discovered a week later. He had not married, had no children, and no relatives shared his last name.

Ray couldn't believe his rescuer hadn't been real. To prove it, his father drove him to Crown Hill Cemetery the next day and showed him the headstone. To their amazement, there was an empty bottle of Heineman's Pink Catawba wine lying next to it! It seems the driver still had a taste for the alcohol that may have been his downfall on the ice all those years ago.

It wasn't only rumrunners who used the lake as a shortcut to Canada. In March 1926, James Phipps, his wife, and three children set out from Leamington, Ontario, to Pelee Island, where Mr. Phipps's mother lived. After spending the night with her, they planned to make the journey back to Leamington, but a morning snowstorm created nearly white-out conditions. Undeterred, Mr. Phipps hustled his family into the car and drove off. Forty-eight hours later, the family still hadn't arrived home. A search party, including an airplane, scoured the region, looking for evidence of holes in the ice or anything to suggest what might have befallen the family. Nothing was found.

Ten days later, on March 21, mysterious lights appeared over Middle Island. Rescuers, convinced the family must have made it to land and built a signal fire, combed the island. But there was no trace, not even a charred piece of wood from a campfire. Sadly, the family was never found.

Around this same time, a man named Lemuel Brown owned the island and had a home near its center. One evening as he gathered wood, he saw a tall flash of light. Convinced it was a column of fire coming from his house, he dropped the wood and ran home to extinguish the flames. When he arrived, the house sat peacefully, with no flames to be seen. Mr. Brown searched the land around the house and found no evidence of fire. He returned to gather the wood he had dropped and saw the same flash of light! Over the years, Mr. Brown witnessed the same column of light many times while on the shore, but always at night, never in daylight.

Gibraltar Island

Gibraltar Island sits at the mouth of Put-in-Bay, acting as a break wall for rough waters when storms churn Lake Erie. It's one reason Commander Perry chose the bay as his base of operations in the War of 1812.

When Mr. De Rivera purchased the Bass Islands, Gibraltar was part of the package deal. In 1864, a man named Jay Cooke wanted the island to build a summer home. Cooke was a successful banker in Philadelphia, and during the Civil War, he pioneered the concept of war bonds. An army with a larger war chest than the enemy stands a better chance of winning. The Union army was running out of cash. Cooke suggested selling bonds to citizens. The purchase price of the bond was like a loan to the government and an investment for the buyer. Citizens bought bonds for one price, and at the end of the bond period (usually sometime after the war), the government paid back the loans with interest. The bonds worked and the Union army finances were secured. It is impossible to say the Union would have lost without Cooke's ingenious idea, but there is no doubt he helped the Union succeed.

"Cooke's Castle," as the summer home is known to locals, still looks over the water almost like a sentry. In its heyday, the home employed a large staff of housekeepers, gardeners, cooks, and butlers. Annabelle Mavis was the teenage daughter of one of the cooks and lived in the servants' quarters with her family. Legend says Annabelle, while not an official employee at the castle, often helped her mother in the kitchens.

Mr. Cooke frequently used couriers to handle messages to and from Gibraltar Island. Often, the couriers came with a message and had to wait several hours, often in the kitchen, while Mr. Cooke wrote a response to be taken back to Put-in-Bay village.

With lots of time on their hands, and with Annabelle often in the kitchen, it was only a matter of time until one messenger fell in love with her. Soon, he gave his love a locket with a photo of himself and a small lock of his hair. Annabelle swore she would never take it off and promised to marry him as soon as she came of age.

As with so many ghost stories, Annabelle's romance does not have a happy ending. One day, as she walked along the bluffs at the shore of the island, a gardener from the castle caught her by surprise. She tried to fight him off, but in the struggle, the locket was ripped from her neck and tumbled onto the rocks below.

When her beau returned, he saw the locket was gone. Assuming she no longer loved him, he turned and left, refusing to listen to her pleas.

Desperate to prove her love, Annabelle searched into the night for her locket. It was all in vain because the locket was never found, nor did the soldier ever return to Gibraltar. Whether Annabelle ever married remains a mystery. Locals at Put-in-Bay village say on calm nights, a woman with a lantern wanders the rocks, still searching for the symbol of the love she lost.

Today, Gibraltar Island is owned by the Ohio State University, where the Franz Theodore Stone Lab is the oldest freshwater biological research station in the United States. If you visit Put-in-Bay, wait for a calm evening, and look to Gibraltar Island for the glow of a lantern held aloft by the ghost of Annabelle Mavis. Maybe someday she will find her locket and be reunited with her courier for eternity.

South Bass Island Lighthouse

At the far west tip of South Bass Island stands the South Bass Lighthouse, erected in 1897. After the end of the Civil War, Lake Erie became a major trade route between the Midwest and the East Coast. Increased ship traffic highlighted a need for safety measures, and because the South Passage between the lighthouses on Green Island and the Marblehead peninsula was especially precarious, the US Lighthouse

Board chose Parker's Point as the location for the new lighthouse.

When it was finished, the light could be seen from fifteen miles away, helping guide ships safely through the South Passage. It operated from May until December, when the lake typically froze over for the winter. It required fuel oil to operate, so it had to be attended to daily.

That was the job of the lighthouse keeper, Harry Riley, the first keeper for the South Bass Island Lighthouse. He was there when the lamp was first lit on July 10, 1897. He and his wife lived in the two-and-a-half-story Queen Anne–style brick house attached to the lighthouse.

A year later, Mr. Riley hired an assistant lightkeeper. Sam Anderson moved into the basement of the lighthouse, where he also kept a rather large collection of live snakes.

Mr. Anderson didn't keep his job long. About a month after he was hired, the island suffered an outbreak of smallpox. Fortunately, cases were mild, and no one died. But Mr. Anderson became so paranoid, he locked himself in the basement with his snakes. Alcohol seemed to be the only thing to calm his fears. It wasn't long before alcohol took its toll.

On the evening of August 31, 1898, Mr. Anderson emerged from his self-imposed quarantine, raving. Accounts differ about whether he was drunk or whether he'd had a mental health crisis. Regardless, the night would be Mr. Anderson's last. His body was recovered from the lake the next morning.

No records document Mr. Anderson's final moments. Some people said he tried to sneak

past quarantine guards and was brought back to the lighthouse but then threw himself over the cliff rather than be cooped up with the snakes again. Others said he wandered outside the lighthouse all night, howling like a wolf or a dog, and fell to his death. Others swear he emerged from his basement, shouted, "God save them all!" and jumped into the lake.

Whether his death was an accident or suicide will never be known. For Mr. Riley, the tragedy of his friend and coworker's death was more than he could take. The day after Mr. Anderson's death, police arrested Mr. Riley when he was discovered wandering around Sandusky raving about racehorses, then they transferred him to the Toledo Asylum for the Insane.

Doctors at the facility evaluated Mr. Riley and determined he was beyond treatment. A month later, he was dead. There are few details about Mr. Riley's symptoms or diagnosis, and mental healthcare was not as advanced in those days. Treatment usually consisted of institutionalizing anyone who did not exhibit "normal" behavior. People could be institutionalized for reasons such as reading, laziness, tobacco use, religious fervor, or being the victim of domestic abuse. Physical reasons included fever, epilepsy, asthma, smallpox, and swelling of limbs.

Today, modern medicine helps us understand the causes for thousands of physical and emotional illnesses and helps us treat them effectively. But that wasn't the case back in the late 1800s.

We may never know whether the men's conditions were related to their work or whether it was simply coincidence. But one thing is certain: an apparition still wanders the property surrounding the lighthouse. Perhaps

Mr. Riley watches over the South Passage, ensuring ships travel safely. Or maybe Mr. Anderson relives the night before his untimely death over and over, as if hoping to change the outcome.

The basement of the lighthouse is another spot for strange phenomena, especially feelings of being watched. Mr. Anderson may have decided the safest place for him to be in the afterlife is in the basement, far from the dangers of smallpox, safe with his snakes. Or maybe the spirits of the snakes still slither along the floor, searching for an escape.

Today, the Ohio State University owns the lighthouse, where there's now a National Oceanic and Atmospheric Association station monitoring the weather on Lake Erie. Tours are offered during the summer tourist season. Whoever, or whatever, may be roaming the lighthouse and its basement, so be sure to go in the daylight. Unless you're up for a ghostly good time searching for specters!

The Put-in-Bay Brewery and Distillery

When Joseph De Rivera realized how mild the climate of the islands was, he created a thriving wine-producing industry. Thanks to Chris and Carl Krueger and Scott Jackson, the island also has a thriving beer brewery and liquor distillery.

The Kruegers and Mr. Jackson bought what had at one time been a small frame shop and dry goods store owned by David Benjamin

Rosenberg, or "Benny" as he was known to friends. Mr. Rosenberg relocated his business several times, eventually buying an old roller rink to convert to a new, larger dry goods store. He owned this until the Great Depression, when he went bankrupt and, like so many others during this difficult time, lost everything. After liquidating all his stock, Mr. Rosenberg took his own life in the storage room of the vacant dry-goods store.

Because he had no living relatives, the building became city property and was eventually turned into the fire department for Put-in-Bay Village. Finally, in 1995, the fire department outgrew the building and sold the property. The new owners began renovations for the brewery immediately.

Renovations alone can't erase history, and sometimes the spirits of a place feel a need to be noticed amid all the change. Take the shadowy woman with flowing hair and dress who haunts the brewery, as an example.

The woman appeared to two waitresses as they worked together on the patio one evening. As the pair rolled silverware into napkins, Kylie Symonds saw the woman appear on the edge of her vision, trying to get her attention. The other waitress, Khloe Zohlgarnain, noticed the customer, too. When they looked up, the spirit vanished. They realized they had seen the same thing at the same time.

Bartender Ken Bodie never saw the vanishing woman, but he recalled seeing a young girl in the hallway near the restrooms. As he walked by, he thought it strange for a child to be unsupervised, so he turned back to ask where her parents were. She was gone! Mr. Bodie isn't the only person to have seen her, but she tends to appear in areas of the brewery without security cameras.

One evening, another employee had a cell phone and managed to capture a supernatural event involving what could have been the young girl. Above the bar sits a small door, about two feet square, which appears to lead nowhere. The employee was recording a video with a friend when the door began to open in the background. Immediately, the employee pivoted the camera to watch the door open all the way. There is nothing behind the door to account for this, and yet it was all captured on video. Though staff try to keep it closed, it still tends to open on its own. Employees like to think the young girl plays hide-and-seek in here.

Even stranger are all the electrical disturbances throughout the brewery. Paranormal investigators attribute this phenomenon to spikes in an area's EMF, or electromagnetic field. The theory is that when a ghost is nearby, it needs energy to manifest itself or its actions, so it pulls electricity from nearby sources, causing phenomena such as flashing lights, cold spots, and power surges.

Daily, usually in the morning, at least one or two lightbulbs pop in the restrooms when the lights are first turned on. Maybe someone thinks it's too early and prefers the dark. Circuit breakers flip on and off. Televisions and phones act up. A speaker mounted on the ceiling above the bar suddenly fell on a bartender's head one evening, even though it had been mounted securely.

Put-in-Bay Brewery sells not just glasses of their beers and ales, but they also sell glass jugs to take home—jugs that used to be kept on a shelf above the beer taps until they began flying off the shelf at random! One staff member watched a glass coffee carafe fly off its base, shattering on the floor. No one was standing near the coffee maker at the time. Nighttime cleaning staff have heard strange noises and watched things fall off shelves for no apparent reason. While the young girl and mystery woman may be behind these events, most employees believe Benny is responsible, because these things tend to happen when someone mentions his name. Mr. Bodie

confirmed this, saying one evening as he was closing the bar, he was hoping Benny would appear and called out to him, egging him on. Apparently, Benny decided enough was enough and slammed the door to the kitchen, rattling it for the next thirty seconds or so. Mr. Bodie apologized, locked up, and went home.

Employees don't talk much about Benny anymore because it only seems to rile him up. If you stop into the brewery for lunch or dinner, maybe you can ask Benny to pop a lightbulb in the restroom or toss something to the floor. Don't be surprised if he takes you up on it and leaves you in the dark!

CHAPTER 9

The Crew's Nest

On the southwest shore of Put-in-Bay stands a sunny, yellow two-story building with lots of windows, a huge covered front porch, and a white picket fence. The cheerful exterior makes The Crew's Nest seem like an unlikely place for all the activity it's known for.

This exclusive private boat club began life in 1875 as the Eagle Cottage Hotel, providing nicely appointed guest rooms for the island's seasonal visitors. After several management changes, the building had fallen into disrepair and was shuttered. Finally, a new owner had a different vision for the classic building. After extensive renovations that maintained the charm of the original architecture, the Crew's Nest opened to the public in 1972, offering a members-only boat club with exclusive docks, a clubhouse, dining room, pool, and bathhouse. Eventually, several more pools, a fitness center, and some tennis and basketball courts were added.

Melinda Myers is the current owner of the boat club, and she has lots of stories to tell. When she was much younger and her father still owned and ran the business, Ms. Myers needed to grab something from the building. It was off-season, so she thought she was alone. Suddenly, she heard footsteps on the floor above. When she searched the second story, it was empty.

Sometime later, Ms. Myers and her sister were sitting in the front room of the club, again in the off-season, putting together Easter baskets. Footsteps sounded above them. Once again, the second floor was empty. This time, there was another witness, so Ms. Myers knew it was not her imagination.

Shortly after her father turned over the business to Ms. Myers, one of her employees complained that the bar staff kept leaving the door to the billiard room open when they closed for the night. The bartenders insisted they never used the door, so to keep the peace, they began overseeing the closing procedures: one person locked the door, and another double-checked it. Nevertheless, when staff opened in the morning, the billiard room door was always ajar. Finally, someone installed a deadbolt, and that solved the problem.

Longtime family friend and former employee Bridge Francis experienced something he couldn't explain one night. At about two in the morning, Mr. Francis and two other men were closing the bar for the night when they heard what sounded like silverware clanking in a room upstairs. Even though the three men were supposed to be the only people in the building, they assumed someone must be upstairs. As Mr. Francis walked up the steps, the clanking grew louder until he stood outside the office door, where the sounds were loudest. The moment he put his head inside to listen, the clanking stopped. Unsettled, the three men decided it was time to leave.

An anonymous staff member remembers walking along the side of the building, looking up, and seeing the outline of a person sitting in a chair in front of one of the windows, even though no one should be in that room. He checked to be certain, and sure enough, no one was upstairs, and no chair sat by the window.

Noises and silhouettes of spirits can sometimes be explained away. It's much harder to explain lights turning on and off or appliances starting with no one to operate them. But employees wonder if they have a trickster, whom they've nicknamed "Spencer," causing all the trouble, such as flipping light switches to leave them in the dark while they work. On several occasions, Spencer has turned on gas stove burners and left them going all night, even after staff double-checked to be sure it was off. One morning, as Ms. Myers and the chef were chatting outside before entering the building, one of the cooks came out to say, "It's happened again," and took them in to show them the flames on the stove.

The most unsettling paranormal event for Ms. Myers happened on a day she cleaned and organized the cluttered attic space. After she'd tidied everything, she came downstairs and found a rubber rat the staff liked to tuck around the building as a joke. Ms. Myers went to the attic stairs and tossed it up. Before she could close the door, it bounced down the stairs again. She thought it was strange because she knew there was nothing on the floor the rat could have bounced against to reverse its direction. She tossed it up again. Again, it came bouncing down the stairs. "Stop it!" she yelled into the attic and lobbed the rat once more. This time, it stayed. Maybe Spencer decided the game wasn't fun anymore.

In the history of the building, there are no tragic stories, nothing to explain the different experiences people have had over the years. One theory is the proximity of the island's original cemetery may be responsible. Just across Victory Street to the west is the Dodge House, another island landmark. Records show the front lawn of this home served as the first cemetery on the island, and many of the casualties of the Battle of Lake Erie were laid to rest here in 1813. It's possible their restless spirits wandered beyond the borders of the cemetery, trying to get closer to their ships, but ended up at the Crew's Nest instead.

In the summer of 2016, a psychic medium came to the Crew's Nest to cleanse the building. Her assessment was different island residents had been popping in to pay a visit or play a prank, but none of the entities intended malice or harm.

Or maybe former owners, employees, and guests simply want to relive their happiest memories of their time on South Bass Island and Put-in-Bay. If you visit the island, be sure to walk by the Crew's Nest and check those upstairs windows. If you see someone in a chair looking out at you, remember they mean no harm. Probably.

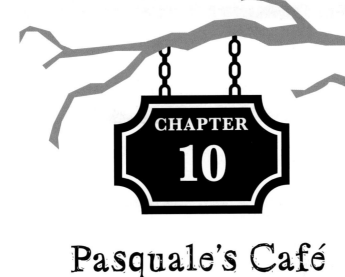

Pasquale's Café

Because of South Bass Island's location near the Canadian Border, it used to have a US Customs office where anyone arriving from Canada stopped to declare any items they brought with them. In the early 1900s, the office was converted to a barbershop that had several owners. The last owner, Bill McCann, was a local handyman around the island before taking over the business, so he knew almost everyone.

His career as a barber allowed him to maintain these connections with the community, and he was often seen through the barbershop window having lively conversations with customers. During quieter moments, he liked to sit in his barber chair and read the paper.

Mr. McCann was also known around town as a violinist, and anyone walking past the barbershop in the evenings might hear lively tunes coming from the apartment above, where the McCann family lived. However, Mrs. McCann didn't enjoy the music as much as the townsfolk, leading Mr. McCann to stash his two violins somewhere in the apartment.

One May afternoon in 1962, a friend passed the barbershop and noticed a lull in customers. He popped his head in to say hello as Mr. McCann read the newspaper, but the old barber said nothing. Thinking he may have fallen asleep, the friend shouted a bit louder. Still no response. Finally, the friend approached the chair, intending to wake the barber. Mr. McCann had died peacefully while catching up on the day's news.

Today, the barber chair sits in the lobby of the Red Moon Saloon. For a brief time, it made its home in the lobby of the Park Hotel, where guests frequently saw it spinning. But witnesses also say age had stiffened the chair, and spinning it was not easy. There's no way a stray breeze could overcome the resistance of the chair. At least, not without some haunted help.

After his death, Mr. McCann's family packed up some of Bill's belongings, but they couldn't find the violins. Several months later, having searched high and low, Mrs. McCann mentioned to her son she was glad he'd found the violins and had played them. She missed her husband's music more than she had realized. But her son insisted the instruments were still missing. Music continued to play in the building for the next twenty years until, during a renovation, the front stairwell was removed to reveal the long-lost violins. Ever since, music no longer floats through the halls of what was to become Pasquale's Café. Now that Mr. McCann's granddaughter Melinda has her grandfather's cherished violins, there may no longer be a need to invite people to search for the source of the music.

But Mr. McCann's spirit isn't at rest yet. John Domer, a former Pasquale's Café manager, says the old barber's phantom likes to play games, especially with ceiling fans and cash registers. On several occasions when the café was closed, with no cross-breeze coming in, Mr. Domer watched the fan blades begin to spin. He kindly greeted the ghost, and the first fan stopped. Then the next one started. Each fan spun in succession like this until Mr. Domer figured Bill was done.

Sometimes, Mr. McCann tinkers with the cash registers. Each register operates by use of a touch screen. If it isn't used for a bit, it goes into "sleep" mode, and the screen dims. Tapping wakes it up, illuminating the screen. But it requires an actual finger to wake up, much like today's cell phones or tablets. Every so often, employees see different cash registers wake from sleep mode, even though no one is near them. Mr. Domer explained a power surge couldn't be the cause because all the registers are on the same circuit and would have all reacted to the surge. But only one register ever comes on at a time.

Mr. McCann was a fixture in the community for nearly a quarter of a century and was happiest doing what he loved in a place he loved. If you believe Mr. Domer, the old barber has stayed close to home, occasionally inspecting changes to his old building and making Pasquale's Café his new haunt.

CHAPTER 11

T&J's Smokehouse

T&J's Smokehouse bar and restaurant began life in 1871 as a grand hotel, welcoming tourists to South Bass Island, and is also the oldest commercial building in Put-in-Bay Village.

Built by Andrew Hunker, the Hunker House Hotel provided luxury for its guests. Indoor plumbing was a relatively new advancement in personal hygiene, and only the wealthiest could afford it. Not only did Hunker House provide private commodes, which most hotels did not, they also had something virtually no other hotel had at the time: a bathtub with plumbing. Perhaps Mr. Hunker saw the four clawfoot tubs in his hotel as a way to attract guests by offering something no one else would have. Today, only one of those original tubs remains in the building.

Hunker House Hotel went through several different owners and names until Thomas Benton Alexander, also known as "T.B.," purchased it in 1908, changing the name to Hotel Crescent. Mr. Alexander was mayor of the village from 1910 to 1913 and then again from 1919 until he died in 1936.

Before this big career change to hotelier and mayor, Mr. Alexander had been a stage actor in Springfield, Ohio, from age twelve until his thirties. When he took charge of the hotel, he brought many posters from his time as an actor and had them plastered to the walls of his new living space and bedroom in the hotel. They remain there to this day.

In 1981, George Stoiber transformed the old hotel into the Crescent Tavern. In 1993, Mr. Stoiber hired a young dishwasher named Bret Klun, who was only eighteen. Mr. Klun worked his way up to general manager and stayed at the Crescent Tavern until 2011.

Mr. Klun is positive something lurks in the building. He used to have his office on the south end of the upstairs hallway. But it always had a "close feeling," he said, which made him uncomfortable. The room also tended to be hot in the summers. So Mr. Klun moved his office to the old poster room, which was larger and cooler. But it was no less spooky.

Occasionally, Mr. Klun heard tapping on the window, but that was not possible because the window was twenty feet off the ground with no tree branches nearby. He couldn't explain what he heard.

Another former employee at the Crescent Tavern, a man nicknamed "Hippie Jerry," says that for a while, he used the poster room as a bedroom. Friends refused to come inside because it felt eerie.

Mr. Klun's employees often complained of feeling they were being watched or had a sense of general unease when walking into certain rooms. Some employees even refuse to walk into several spaces in the building, including the poster room.

Banging doors, cold spots, and creepy feelings are the least of the experiences Mr. Klun and his employees have had. One evening after closing time, one of his staff was mopping the floors in the dining area when he heard a clatter behind him. He turned to find one of the stands the waitstaff used to put trays of food down had been set up in the middle of the room. The employee assumed it was a prank, even though no one was around. He folded the stand, put it away, and continued mopping. About fifteen minutes later, the sound returned. When he turned, the stand was again set up in the middle of the room. Once more, the employee folded the stand and put it away. About an hour later, as he finished cleaning, it happened one last time. Instead of putting the stand away, the employee put down his mop, walked out, and never returned.

During this same period, longtime island resident John Domer, the manager at Pasquale's Café in the early 1990s, was at work one evening when a woman came into the café asking if there were any openings for a waitress. She had been working at the Crescent Tavern, mostly during the breakfast shift. Occasionally, she worked the dinner shift until closing. One of the closing duties for the waitstaff was to prepare for the breakfast shift by laying out placements, napkins, and silverware, then adding jam, jelly, sugar, and creamer packets to the tables. The night before she arrived at Pasquale's Café to ask for a job, she had worked the closing shift at Crescent, and the only other person working was prepping the kitchen for the next shift. She said she was nearly finished with all her tasks when she realized she needed more supplies. She went to the storage room and returned about thirty seconds later. Everything she had prepared— napkins, silverware, jam, and sugar packets— had been returned to their original shelves and bins. She knew this was impossible because it had taken her almost fifteen minutes to put everything in place, yet it only took thirty seconds for someone, or something, to put everything back. She marched to the kitchen, told her co-worker goodnight, and said she wouldn't be back.

In 2011, the final transfer of ownership and name change took place. Brothers Tim and Josh Niese refurbished Mr. Stoiber's tavern to create a western-style barbecue restaurant and bar. Not only did the Niese brothers buy some historic architecture, but lots of paranormal phenomena came with it. Tim realized something was happening shortly after he and Josh bought the tavern. As Tim worked on some renovation projects on the first floor, he heard what he assumed were a construction crew members' footsteps on the wooden floors above him. But when he stepped outside a few minutes later, the entire crew was outside, nowhere near the house. None of them had been inside when Tim heard the footsteps.

This wasn't the only incident Tim had while renovating. The building had several heavy wooden swinging doors. A breeze might be able to move the doors about an inch, but they were much too heavy to blow open or closed on their own. While working nearby, he heard one of the doors open and close, as if a person had walked through. On this day, no other renovation crew were on site, so Tim was quite alone in the place.

Tim and Josh's nephew witnessed some activity in the old place, too. As the brothers and their nephew walked past the building one day, the young man pointed to an upstairs window where he swore he saw someone. But the building wasn't open to the public yet, and there were no work crews inside. Tim and Josh's nephew isn't the only one who has seen someone in the windows upstairs. Every so often, employees will notice a face peering down from the second story on the street below. But whenever they have gone to investigate, no one is there.

A former janitor in T&J's Smokehouse is sure T.B. Alexander still roams the halls. One evening, as the janitor mopped the bar area after closing, he looked up to see the reflection of a man in the mirror above the bar. The man appeared to be in his sixties or seventies and wore an outdated suit, even though it was the middle of summer. Without turning, the janitor told the man the bar was closed. But the man remained on the barstool as if waiting for someone to pour him a beverage. This time, the janitor turned to say something, but the man vanished, just like that. It wasn't until later the janitor saw the posters upstairs and realized the man in the mirror had been none other than T.B. Alexander himself.

Perhaps the face in the windows belongs to T.B. Alexander, who used to enjoy his bird's-eye view from the second story as he surveyed guests coming and going from his hotel. And perhaps he wanted to check on the bar to make sure everyone was treating his building with respect. He must have been satisfied because he caused no trouble.

Even if Mr. Alexander isn't the type to cause trouble, T&J's Smokehouse does have a little prankster on the premises. Bartender Kelsey Arnold is convinced it's a little boy. During one of her shifts, she walked down the hallway near the restrooms and heard a little boy's laughter coming from the men's room, followed by sounds of the electric hand dryer. But no one was in the men's room. Staff have named the boy "Petey," and they say he frequently activates the dryers in the men's room, sometimes even when there are witnesses to see them turn on by themselves.

Another employee, Blake, shared an experience he had when he brought his young son to work before the restaurant opened. When it was time to go, Blake called for his son, who had wandered upstairs. The boy mentioned he'd been playing upstairs with a friend. Because no one else should have been in the building, Blake checked to make sure no strangers had gotten upstairs, but no one was there.

Another time, Blake had gone into the storeroom shortly before the restaurant renovations were complete. Everything had been organized, neatly arranged, and shelves and bins labeled. But when Blake entered the room, all the labels were on the floor.

Was it Petey the Prankster again? And who is Petey, anyway? Local lore says the child is likely the spirit of a four-year-old boy who died while in one of Andrew Hunker's luxury bathtubs. Records and archives don't provide a name for the little fellow, so Petey will have to do. Whoever he is, and whether he is also responsible for doors opening and closing, tray stands mysteriously appearing in the center of the room, or undoing all the work the waitress did to prepare for the breakfast shift the next morning, the lad seems to intend no harm and simply wants to play as he did when he was still alive.

If you visit T&J's Smokehouse, maybe you'll hear Petey playing with the hand dryers in the restroom. Or perhaps you can look up and wave to T.B. Alexander as he watches over his former business. Just be sure to look over your shoulder now and then. You never know if one of them might be behind you.

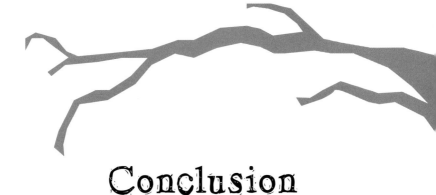

Conclusion

Put-in-Bay and South Bass Island have a long history, and when you walk along the bluffs near the shore, visit the Peace Memorial, wander the streets filled with old homes, hotels, and restaurants, or roam the grounds of the lighthouse, now you can imagine what life was like for the brave souls who explored, settled, fought, lived, and died here. You can picture the smoking cannons of the USS *Niagara* or watch in your mind as the USS *Lawrence* sinks below the surface of Lake Erie. And if you happen to see something else, like a barber chair spinning on its own or a toy bouncing down the stairs, you'll know it's only the phantoms of the bay saying hello.

Jay Whistler was born on Halloween and grew up in a haunted house. She loves listening to ghost stories, whether real or imagined, and willingly explores haunted places on her travels across the country and around the globe. Even so, she will always be afraid of the dark. The boring part is that Jay has her MFA in writing from Vermont College of Fine Arts.

Check out some of the other Spooky America titles available now!

Spooky America was adapted from the creeptastic Haunted America series for adults. Haunted America explores historical haunts in cities and regions across America. Each book chronicles both the widely known and less-familiar history behind local ghosts and other unexplained mysteries. Here's more from *Haunted Put-in-Bay* author William G. Krejci: